Migration and the Church in East Asia

Migration and the Church in East Asia

Paul Woods

regnum

First published 2020 by Regnum Books International

This book is an abridged version of Paul Woods' *Theologising Migration* (Oxford: Regnum, 2015), with thanks to David Cranston for his editorial work. The original research was conducted in 2013.

Regnum is an imprint of the Oxford Centre for Mission Studies
St. Philip and St. James Church
Woodstock Road, Oxford OX2 6HR, UK
www.ocms.ac.uk/regnum

09 08 07 06 05 04 03 7 6 5 4 3 2 1

British Library Cataloguing in Publication Data. A catalogue record for this book is available from the British Library.

ISBN: 978-1-5064-8403-7

eBook ISBN: 978-1-5064-8404-4

Typeset in Candara by Words by Design.

Photo by Pawel Czerwinski on Unsplash.

The publication of this volume is made possible through the financial assistance of Evangelisches Missionswerk.

Distributed by 1517 Media in the US, Canada, India, and Brazil

Contents

Introduction

Migration has been described as 'one of the defining issues of the twenty-first century'. The International Organization for Migration claims that migration is 'an essential, inevitable and potentially beneficial component of the economic and social life of every country and region'. Any phenomenon which is described in such striking terms deserves the attention and response of the church, and for Christians, migration is fundamentally about people.

In the secular world, much attention has already been paid to migration. In some countries, migration is seen as a good thing, bringing in new people with skills and money. In other locations the so-called *Kleenex* workers - use once and throw away – are used and abused to carry out tasks which locals do not wish to do. Migrants may be seen as people who quickly adopt the standards and life-style of the host country and culture, or alternatively as outsiders who endanger the *status quo*.

This theological study is orientated to migration in six territories in East Asia: Hong Kong, Singapore, Malaysia, Korea, Taiwan, and Japan. Detailed studies of migration in the region have yet to be undertaken by the Christian community and this complex phenomenon merits comprehensive research by the church, theologians, and missiologists.

Migration *is* people, moving as never before. All who travel across borders are made in God's image and precious to him. Their presence represents a challenge and an opportunity to churches to bring people of no belief or another belief into environments where Christians live and practise their faith. Because migration undermines the old dichotomies of home outreach and foreign mission, we need to apply the Great Commission of Matthew 28 and the Great Commandment of Matthew 22 in new and creative ways.

Migration and Globalisation

While migration may be seen as a relatively recent phenomenon, people have been moving in large numbers for thousands of years. Consider the movements of Han people into the region south of the Yangtze in the time of Confucius or the domination of Western Europe by the Celts and their later fragmentation by the Roman Empire. The latter is an early form of globalisation in that it involved a trade language and exchange of goods across a very large area. The Silk Road was another incarnation, connecting East and West for trade and the interchange of ideas.

There have been similar ebbs and flows on every continent throughout history, but what is significant about modern migration is its speed and scope. Migrants can travel now around the globe in 24 hours. Flights are cheap and so is communication by phone or internet. Gone are the gradual movement of people over years and the gentle integration into local cultures. The ability of people to move rapidly means that they come with their cultures and languages intact and in many cases see no need to learn local languages or customs other than for survival or business. Modern migration may therefore involve cross-cultural tensions or clashes, as people move quickly and often in significant numbers, groups of culturally and ethnically different people suddenly appearing in locations where their distinctiveness may not be appreciated.

When migration occurs from poorer to richer countries, it is subject to immigration policies set by host nations for their own purposes. A citizen of a rich, democratic nation may travel around the world with comparative ease, perhaps needing a visa here and there, but for a person whose journey is motivated by financial need or hardship the situation can be very different. The vast majority of migrants do not enjoy the benefits of a globalising, interconnected world. For them, movement across borders is difficult and degrading and they may find themselves at the bottom of any social stratification in their destination country. These days a greater variety of people travel, but the governing criteria are wealth and citizenship. Migration is not a level playing field and huge injustices remain.

The Rise of East Asia in a Multipolar World

In the decades since the colonial era many East Asian countries have shown rapid growth. Singapore has boomed, while Malaysia has made impressive progress and Thailand has made huge strides. The Philippines and Indonesia have not performed as well, while other members of the Association of South East Asian Nations (ASEAN) continue to recover from or cope with communism and corruption.

In parallel with the economic rise and increasingly powerful voice of Asian nations, the church has come of age and there is strong interest in cross-cultural mission. Where the church is free to exist, it reaches out and sends missionaries abroad. In Singapore and Korea for example, cross-cultural mission has developed in step with church growth.

Changing Church and Changing Missions in East Asia

In the past, mission was understood primarily as western people taking the gospel to the rest of the world, but now East Asians are ministering within and outside their region. This is part of the maturation of the church and the mission endeavour that accompanies it.

However, whereas ministry to foreigners, especially students, is well established in many western countries, it is perhaps less so in East Asia. In addition, whether in East or West, migrant ministry tends to be reactive, theologically under-informed, and insufficiently integrated with other mission work.

In many parts of the world, outreach to migrants is slowly gaining acceptance as a viable ministry, but often falls between two stools. Some people do not think of it as 'mission' because there is no need for the missionary to travel abroad, but others feel it is not 'outreach' because that term traditionally refers to local evangelism to one's own people. This flawed conceptualisation can be seen in the policies of churches and mission organisations who have fallen into the traditional home-field dichotomy and need help understanding a changing world and the implications for the Great Commission.

Although western churches are generally more advanced in ministry to migrants, it is fair to say that a robust and multifaceted theology of ministry has yet to emerge anywhere in the evangelical world. A review of websites of Bible and mission colleges in the West reveals a disturbing absence of both a theology of migrant ministry and specialised academic courses. Given that the engine of theological research is still primarily in the West, it is not surprising that this lack of theological engagement is mirrored in East Asia's churches and seminaries.

A further difficulty is that migrants are often needy and vulnerable, socially, emotionally, and financially. For many conservative evangelicals, social concern may be perceived as liberal theology and a dilution of the orthodox spiritual gospel. Integral mission and social justice need to be strengthened in the East Asian evangelical scene.

Although the evangelical world has yet to develop a robust theology of migrant ministry, there have been significant efforts under the International Catholic Migration Commission and broader Protestant groupings such as the World Council of Churches. In recent statements Pope Benedict has appealed to the church and the world to take care of migrants and has described migration as an opportunity rather than a problem.

The clear concern of Catholic and ecumenical Protestantism for the stranger and the disadvantaged should speak to evangelicalism. There is a need for a theology of migrant ministry in East Asia which is derived from the scriptures and addresses the responsibilities of Christians in the host societies to which migrants come.

Migration in East Asia

The World Migration Report of 2008 states that at least 200 million people live and work in a country other than their own. Half are women, the majority of whom work as temporary labour in the Middle East and East Asia.

Currently, Europe and Central Asia host more than 70 million migrants, North America 45 million, and Asia 25 million. The value of remittances sent home by migrant workers is around US$350 billion. In poorer countries, this plays a significant role in the income of families and the nation. In 2002, just under 10% of the Philippines GDP came from migrant workers.

Migrant labourers constitute 3% of the global labour force and take on a wide range of employment opportunities, from the highly educated and experienced white-collar expatriate, down through skilled contract labour in construction and manufacturing, to semi-skilled and unskilled workers. In many countries the highly skilled labour force can obtain work permits and even permanent residence with comparative ease whereas semi-skilled workers usually have to return home on completion of fixed length contracts.

Most intra-Asian migrants are on temporary employment, and in the more prosperous nations local people are increasingly unwilling to do the so-called 3-D jobs, ‘dirty, dangerous, and demeaning’.

Country Overview

Singapore

In Singapore migration is tightly controlled and policy is designed to combine economic development with social harmony for the nation. Highly skilled foreigners can bring their families to live and settle, while manual and low skilled workers are less welcome, unable to bring their families or apply for permanent residence. A female domestic worker who becomes pregnant is returned to her home country almost immediately. This difference in treatment has led to the term ‘bifurcated’ for the foreign labour system.

Malaysia

Malaysia controls unskilled foreign labour tightly and visas are given for short, fixed terms. When the economy is doing well foreign workers are relatively welcome, but in times of economic difficulty they may be encouraged and even required to leave.

In West Malaysia, out of a total of 1,200,000 legal short term contract foreign workers 60% are Indonesian, with one fifth of the total Malaysian workforce made up of foreign nationals. Migration in Malaysia is complex and notoriously difficult to document due to the porous border with Thailand and the ease with which Indonesians enter the country from Sumatra. Current estimates suggest that there may be more than 400,000 illegal workers in manufacturing and construction.

Malaysia now plays host to around 50,000 foreign students at the tertiary level, around 2% of the global total from neighbouring countries including China. The Malaysian government set a target of 100,000 overseas students for 2010.

Hong Kong

Hong Kong's immigrant population is also bifurcated: a small portion of highly paid migrants comes from developed countries such as the US and Japan, while a large portion of low-paid migrant labour is from Mainland China, the Philippines and Thailand.

Hong Kong gives visas for around 60,000 foreign domestic workers each year, and also welcomes around 16,000 foreign professionals. Among the quarter million foreign domestic helpers in Hong Kong two thirds are from the Philippines and the most of the remainder from Indonesia. Where necessary, labour is brought in from China on a strictly short-term basis. There are very small numbers of foreign students in Hong Kong and increasing numbers of Mainland Chinese live and work in Hong Kong.

Taiwan

Taiwan has large numbers of migrant labourers in its manufacturing and construction sectors and smaller amounts of foreign domestic workers and caregivers.

Foreign workers come from the Philippines, Vietnam, Indonesia, and Thailand; half of all registered migrant Thai workers in the world work in Taiwan. In 2006, a quarter of the Vietnamese workers in the country worked in factories, while most of the remainder were domestic helpers and caregivers.

The national drive to a more knowledge-based economy has also increased openness to foreign professionals. There is a small number of international students.

Korea

In recent decades Korea has become an industrial powerhouse. A very significant change in labour policy in 2003 saw the acceptance of unskilled foreign workers, who are mostly employed in manufacturing and construction, with smaller numbers in the service (including private nursing) and agricultural sectors. Labour regulations explicitly forbid the entrance of family members, to dissuade foreign workers from staying permanently.

In 2002, the largest group of immigrants in the country was Mainland Chinese, but more than 12,000 Vietnamese women go to Korea as brides every year, with four times as many foreign brides as foreign grooms.

Japan

Although Japan has had economic difficulties for some time and has seen rising unemployment, the number of migrant workers and permanent residents is increasing. Among Mainland Chinese alone, 70,000 have permanent resident status in Japan, which is viewed with growing concern by many Japanese. There appears to be no special category for unskilled foreign labour in the construction sector, while around 300,000 work in manufacturing. Many who enter the country as temporary visitors end up in various forms of illegal employment.

Japan operates a policy under which foreign workers come for vocational training. Foreign trainees are found in manufacturing, agriculture, and nursing, and many suffer significant exploitation.

Major Sending Countries

As early as 2003, Mainland China had already sent 2.45 million migrant workers abroad. The bifurcation or double standard in receiving territories such as Hong Kong and Singapore is also found at the sending end. Mainland Chinese going abroad for extended periods are either the highly qualified who may decide to live abroad indefinitely, or unskilled or semi-skilled labourers who work in tough circumstances to earn more than they can in China.

Most Vietnamese migrants are unskilled contract labourers from relatively poor rural areas who work in domestic service, construction and manufacturing. The majority of Indonesians working abroad are female, the top destinations being Saudi Arabia and Malaysia.

In 2003, around one quarter of Filipinos working overseas were in manufacturing, transport, or manual labour. Another quarter are described as entertainers and just under 20% work as domestic helpers. Thailand still sends a significant numbers of migrant workers abroad.

Migration Theory

Overview

In their 2003 seminal work *The Age of Migration*, Stephen Castles and Mark Miller argued that movements of people are normally based on pre-existing relationships between sending and receiving territories, which may exist for reasons of history, politics, culture or trade. As examples, they mention people flows from the Caribbean to former colonial powers and connections between France and North Africa.

They suggest that the migration process involves different structures at different levels. Macro-structures operate between nation states in the areas of economics and policy, while at the other end of the scale micro-structures facilitate migration primarily through personal and family relationships. The latter provide a safety net for new arrivals and an element of home-from-home in the host country. In most situations a meso-structure of middlemen and brokers helps meet the demand for semi-skilled labour. Decent companies and reliable brokers are precious, and their details are shared among prospective migrants to maintain links between people in the home and destination countries. In Asia, the extended family often selects a young person to work abroad. In agricultural societies, the greater physical strength of men and the greater financial reliability of women, especially in the matter of sending remittances, mean that young women are often sent abroad.

In many East Asian cities, diaspora people run small shops selling foodstuffs and other products from their home countries. Although they exist primarily for commercial purposes, they often serve as *de facto* cultural outposts and become magnets for migrants.

A Cultural and Historical Sketch of the Host Nations

Overview

Because migration creates physical, cultural, and social distance, it is important to consider not only the migration process but also the host territories for migrants. When churches undertake mission to migrants the number of Christians in contact with foreigners is usually greater than the number of traditional cross-cultural missionaries sent abroad. Migrants may meet a relatively larger cross-section of church members, attend church events, and even visit church members' homes. Ministry to migrants is challenging because the church community is 'on display' while remaining a product of the broader culture. It is important to understand the attitudes and worldview of the host nations.

The following anecdote illustrates this point. A female church member met her pastor while at church with her domestic helper. The man shook hands with the church member enthusiastically and noticed the helper but did not even offer to shake her hand. The church member confessed that few Christians are willing to spend time with foreign domestic workers or contract labourers even in the church or among believers. It would be unlikely for traditional missionaries in the field to harbour such attitudes and let them be seen; mission at home has particular challenges of its own.

Of the six territories, those in the North, Korea, Japan, Hong Kong, and Taiwan,) are effectively linguistically and culturally monolithic. This is in contrast to the two nations in the South, Singapore and Malaysia, which are ethnically diverse. In all six territories, the church is dominated by Chinese, Koreans, or Japanese and the principal shared philosophical paradigm of Confucianism has influenced the church, including its attitudes to migrants. Furthermore, all three cultures have demonstrated isolationism and ethnocentrism. At the same time, the six territories share experiences of migration, colonialism, and alienation which might suggest a relative openness and compassion towards migrants.

The Recent History of the Six Territories as it Relates to Migration

Singapore is an immigrant nation; many of the Chinese and Indians and even some of the Malay people are comparatively recent arrivals in the island, although the vast majority of the dominant Chinese group are descendants of people who came to Singapore from South China in the late nineteenth and early twentieth centuries. The island was a British colony from 1819 until 1963, becoming independent of Malaysia in 1965, and suffered ruthless Japanese rule during the Second World War. It might be thought that Singapore's own immigration heritage and its dual experience of colonisation from the British and Japanese would bring empathy for the outsider, the Other, but such concern is not obvious in the literature.

Like Singapore, Malaysia is a former British colony, also occupied by the Japanese during the Second World War. Since independence, political power has been in the hands of the Malay majority, while business belongs very much to the Chinese. Successive Malaysian administrations have favoured the indigenous Malay people and alienated the large Chinese minority. Creeping Islamicisation and the attendant pressure on what is predominantly a Chinese church make the Malaysian Christians feel doubly exposed. It is not clear from the literature whether these pressures have resulted in greater openness to migrants among Malaysian Christians, but there is now a small but significant work among migrant labourers in Malaysia.

Hong Kong is overwhelmingly Chinese. It was colonised by the British from 1842 until 1997 and invaded by the Japanese in the 1940s. In the early 1950s, after the communists came to power in China, huge numbers of people moved to Hong Kong from the Mainland. The Hong Kong people and the church have a double experience of alienation, through colonisation and migration. Since the return of Hong Kong to China in 1997, many local people, while rejoicing in their Chinese-ness, remain suspicious of a communist government which does not understand them and is culturally and linguistically rather distant. One might hope that migrants would find compassion in such a society.

Taiwan has been populated by two large waves of Chinese immigration from the Mainland. The first was the gradual movement of thousands from Fujian Province during the Qing dynasty (1644-1911) and the second the traumatic exile to the island of the nationalist Kuomintang Party of Chiang Kai-shek as they lost the civil war to Mao's communists in 1949.

Foreign colonisation is also part of Taiwan's history. The Dutch and the Spanish ruled the island in the sixteenth and seventeenth centuries, and for the first half of the twentieth it was a Japanese colony. This experience of oppression and vulnerability was followed almost immediately by years of tension and intimidation between Taiwan and Mainland China. The heritage of alienation and vulnerability is strong in the island and one wonders how this might affect attitudes to migrants among the general population and in the church.

Like Taiwan, Korea was dominated by Japan for the first half of the twentieth century. The Japanese colonial rulers set out to eradicate Korean culture and turn the populace into Japanese people. This followed centuries of Chinese linguistic, cultural, and philosophical influence on the Korean peninsula. Many in South Korea are sympathetic to their oppressed cousins in the North, and some remember the North Korean and Chinese invasion of 1950, which pushed democratic forces right to the southern tip of South Korea. Again, there is a history of vulnerability and oppression at the hands of outsiders.

Finally, Japan is the country that has suffered the least at the hands of foreign powers or due to mass dislocation. The Japanese have lived in their own land for centuries and were never colonised. However, the nation was defeated by foreign forces in 1945 and suffered two nuclear attacks. After the war, the Americans occupied the country and rewrote the constitution, bringing huge social change and altering the status of the emperor.

Each nation has experienced dislocation of one kind or another, which may suggest a heightened concern for the migrant. On the other hand, this experience of Otherness, coupled with nation building in the modern era, may also contribute to a more inward-looking, defensive attitude.

The Underlying Worldview of the Six Host Nations

The rough characterisation of western cultures as individualist and Asian as collectivist is well known; in Western cultures the main boundary is between individuals, while in East Asian cultures it is between in-group and out-group.

A central factor in the East Asian worldview is the extended family. In traditional Chinese thinking, each member has to work together for the good of the whole. Confucianism takes the extended family as the basic social unit, upon which all others, including the nation, are modelled. Such is the importance of loyalty to the family bloodline that if there is tension between a man's wife and his parents, it is sometimes expected that the man side with his parents rather than his wife. Good and bad may be defined by their effect on the family or clan, and for Confucians virtues such as 'propriety, truthfulness, justice, the empire, the people, or even humaneness itself' may take second place to a higher principle of filial piety. One should place blood ties above the 'higher' ideals of humanity, even to the point of abandoning these higher ideals if their realisation endangers the practice of family duties. A person derives his identity partly from the ancestors and their worship preserves the unity and centrality of the family as it connects the living to the dead.

A closely related concept is the self, different in Confucian and western thought. In Confucian cultures, self lies primarily in the realisation of one's culturally prescribed, functional roles and relationships with others, and the virtue of humaneness (*ren*) comes primarily from a relationship between two people.

For Confucius and his followers, social order and harmony were vital, and in Confucian thought belonging and responsibility are tightly linked. Because Confucianism emphasises hierarchy and obligation, and family and other close relationships, the position of those without a close connection to a member of the host community could be precarious.

The Confucian 'five relationships' is a general framework for the management of relationships in society, between 'ruler and minister, father and son, husband and wife, elder and younger brothers, and between friends'. All five contain moral and mutual elements, although each also includes an inherent superior-inferior distinction, except for that between friends. In theory, in Confucianism there is a two way responsibility; ruler and ruled have obligations to each other. Practically, the system is asymmetric and those at the lower end of a relationship have more and heavier obligations to those above them. The five relationships establish stratified obligations and hierarchy, and the belief that society works best when each person fulfils his or her role restricts social mobility and disenfranchises outsiders

Migrants do not fit into established relationship structures and may thus be devalued and their personhood undermined. The concept of family loyalty may also push the foreigner out. This has consequences for poorer workers doing 3D jobs, foreign brides, and students. The diminished responsibility for those with greater power is in marked contrast to the 'absolutes on which to combat injustice' of the biblical worldview.

The Migration Experience

People migrating in East Asia encounter issues of racism and intolerance as well as identity and belonging, and these need to be understood as part of any theological and missiological response to migration.

Migrants face a profound disturbance of identity, hoping to belong to a society which they may find is not welcoming. East Asian government policies exclude permanent residence and most migrants have no expectation of belonging to the host country. Under these circumstances, belonging to some entity in the host country is important because Asians locate their identity by group membership and distinctions between groups are clearer than in the West.

The process of moving from one country to another causes huge pressures on people. Migrants experience anxiety about their own situation and worry about loved ones, especially when the aim is to earn higher salaries and provide for the future of dependants back home. Migrant workers suffer significant amounts of abuse and maltreatment, with the added pressure of sexual abuse or intimidation for women.

Migrants can suffer mental or emotional stress due to loneliness and lack of self-esteem; some develop ulcers and suicides do occur. When large numbers of men go abroad, especially in groups, there is a greater likelihood of alcohol and drug abuse, as well as involvement with prostitutes. Women may face abuse and exploitation, unwanted pregnancies, and the heartbreak of caring for someone else's child rather than their own. Many are engaged in 3D jobs or work very long hours in domestic service. Safety standards are not only lax but also rarely applied to 'Kleenex' workers (use once and throw away) who are simply not as important as locals.

Migration affects not only the migrant but also the family left behind. A migrant worker in a host country often means an absent parent in the home country. The consequences of an absent father can be serious; children may grow up without male presence and role models and women's burdens become heavier as they play the role of father as well as mother. When women leave a family, the children grow up motherless or with a domestic helper or relative as caregiver. The needs of families in richer nations such as Singapore or Taiwan may cause family fragmentation in a chain, as a woman leaves a poorer country to work as a foreign domestic worker, requiring another woman in the home country to move from her home, partially or completely, to look after the children of the one who has gone abroad.

While international law guarantees the human and legal rights of migrant workers, there is a discrepancy between what international agreements specify and the situation on building sites and in private homes across the world. Serious human rights violations are not uncommon. Migrants in East Asia are often relatively unskilled and uneducated and not used to defending their cause and demanding their rights. They are especially vulnerable because they are not citizens of the countries in which they work, may have problems with language and culture, and have little idea of their rights or how legal systems work. They may also have to deal with discrimination and intimidation.

It is disturbing that in many countries domestic service is not covered by employment law and often undertaken without the protection of contracts. While some foreign domestic workers are treated like family members, the situation of others approaches slavery. Because they usually work and live in a private house it is almost impossible to monitor their lives, treatment at the hands of employers, and living conditions.

One quarter of the maids in Singapore have no days off (when the research was carried out) and many exist in subservience. Human Rights Watch suggests that psychological abuse is almost universal for foreign domestic workers around the world. In addition, they suffer food deprivation, sexual abuse at the hands of male employers, and enforced isolation from their compatriots. Many lose money to employers and maid agencies, particularly when needing medical care or changing employers for reasons beyond their control, such as abuse.

Physical violence is common, as are forced confinement and denial of access to telephones. Many domestic workers have no place to sleep, often getting a few hours rest on the floor, under a table, and even on stairs.

Abuse of domestic helpers has also been found within the Christian community. One irate blog from a waiter describes a group of Christians having a long and expensive meal while the domestic helper was not given any food or water all night and had to look after a child for the whole evening. Another blog spoke of Muslim girls forced to look after employers' children at church on Sundays instead of being given a day off. Even Bible college students have defended employers who grant domestic helpers only one day off per month; when confronted with God's requirement for one day off per week some argued that this 'is a different situation' and that those who advocate a weekly Sabbath 'do not understand'.

In response, Michael Loh, a Methodist from Singapore, has written a short but powerful article entitled *Maid abuse: One Christian's response*. Writing as a Christian to other Christians, he summarises foreign domestic workers' circumstances in Singapore, quoting a comment he once overheard: 'Oh, Indonesian maids? They are relatively low-maintenance types. One fried egg and a plate of rice would make them happy.' Quoting from Hebrews 13:1-2, he asks his fellow believers, 'Would you let an angel eat only instant noodle? Would you shout at an angel? Would you exclude an angel from celebrations at home?'

He asks fellow believers to treat their 'home helpers' well, discouraging the use of the term 'maid'. He asks employers to be realistic in their expectations, because the domestic worker is in a foreign culture and has needs of her own. He urges church members not to force their helpers to fulfil the roles of parents and tutors as well as domestic factotums. His exhortation is heartening:

> *Accept the maid as someone who is now a part of your family life – ask about her family; every so often, ask to find out if everything's all right. Remember significant dates in her life such as her birthday, wedding anniversary, etc. Celebrating your own birthday? Include her in the celebration. Check if she needs help sending stuff home. Small gestures go a long way and are edifying.*

It is encouraging to hear this almost lone voice inside the evangelical community. It is sad that such reminders of basic humanity are needed among well-read, educated, cosmopolitan Christians in a country where the church has existed for more than a century. The practical and theological issues raised by Loh's short article relate to Confucian concepts of belonging and the responsibility of Christians to Others. They also confirm that mission at home, as opposed to the sending out of cross-cultural workers, involves a much broader section of church people. Indeed, Loh claims: 'Nothing is a more powerful evangelical tool than the way you live your life. At home, your maid sees you as you are, warts and all. How Christian are you at home? Are you, who enjoy God's generosity and blessings, magnanimous and kind – and above all, human and humane?'

The vulnerability of the non-citizen is very evident in the case of foreign domestic workers, and we are reminded of the OT prescriptions about foreigners in ancient Israel.

Contract Labourers

Foreign contract labourers are important to many economies in the region. Workers from China, Thailand, India, Indonesia and other countries usually secure two or three year contracts to earn higher salaries and send money home. Employment is usually found through brokers, who connect sources of labour in poorer countries with construction projects or factories in richer ones. The initial costs for a migrant labourer can be high, including flights, fees, bonds, and insurance, and it is common for half of a foreign worker's total salary in a richer country to be eaten up by the debt he or she incurred by going abroad to work.

Like domestic workers, foreign labourers often work in difficult conditions and for long hours without overtime pay, some even seven days per week. A recent traffic accident in Singapore highlighted the apparent difference between the value of a migrant worker's life and that of a local or a highly-skilled expatriate. It was asked why those driving in cars are required to wear seatbelts, while foreign labourers often ride in the back of lorries at high speed without any safety measures at all.

Foreign workers are often billeted in converted shipping containers at the construction site where they work. These usually have basic furniture and an air-conditioning unit fixed onto the outside, and are often overcrowded and unhygienic. Facilities for washing, showering, laundering, and cooking are often inadequate. It is common to see workers' clothes hanging to dry on semi-constructed buildings. Various collections of *YouTube* videos portray these poor living conditions.

In an article in Malaysia's *New Straits Times*, a trade union leader claimed that foreign workers are treated like slaves, with only verbal work agreements and no idea of their rights, their passports held by the employer. If a foreign worker registers a complaint against his Malaysian company, his employment pass is usually cancelled immediately and the worker becomes an illegal. His only recourse is to pay a fine to the immigration department while his case is investigated. Similar conditions are seen in Taiwan and Amnesty International's report on Korea contains other harrowing stories, including one of a Chinese man who froze to death on the street as he struggled to make ends meet because his salary was not paid.

Foreign Brides

Women who marry men from richer East Asian nations and move to those countries often experience alienation, prejudice, and loss of culture and self-esteem. Many of these marriages are arranged through brokers who help rich men choose a bride in a country like Vietnam, where the young women have little understanding of life in the husband's country and very often cannot even communicate with him. The young women can be trapped, feeling vulnerable and lonely, with huge emotional needs. Divorce and the return of the young women to their home country are increasingly common.

International Students

International students in East Asia usually undertake tertiary education in a foreign language such as English, Chinese, or Korean. This causes culture shock as students need to negotiate a new academic environment and relate to a new group of friends, colleagues, and possibly competitors, while dealing with issues such as food, accommodation and part-time work.

All these issues merit a kingdom response from God's community. The biblical theme of wholeness or *shalom* comes to mind, and we should ask, 'What is *shalom* for migrant workers and through what channels might it be mediated?' The nature of the response is important: does the community of faith simply reach out and provide assistance at arm's length, or does it 'reach out to reach in' and attempt to embrace migrants as part of itself?

Advocacy for Migrants in East Asia

There are people and organisations who care for those on the move. Migrant organisations are strong in Hong Kong, Taiwan, Japan, and Korea, where they are legally permitted to exist and carry out their activities, but weaker in Singapore and Malaysia, where they must operate carefully and avoid what might be taken as political activity. Among Christian faith-based organisations, the Catholic Church leads the way in responding to migration.

Although recent years have seen an increase in church-based evangelism to foreign labourers as well as services and fellowships for foreign domestic workers in Singapore and Malaysia, the theological rationale for the ministry is still weak and much gospel work neglects context and does not prepare people for the return home.

In addition, many evangelical churches see their task as the proclamation of the 'spiritual gospel', with very little holistic care or worker advocacy. An integrated approach is needed, which takes seriously the needs of migrants and the nature of migration. Across the region there is a clear reflection of the classic (American) liberal-fundamentalist divide; some Christian groups minister to the body and advocate social justice without mention of spiritual transformation, while others present blunt, context-free Bible messages about 'God, Jesus, and sin'. These concepts are often totally alien to migrant workers from China, Thailand, and India, and misunderstood by those from Indonesia and the Philippines! Such messages *seem* to have little immediate usefulness for those who hear them and have no manifestation of social justice.

Existing Scholarship Relevant to Migration

Introduction

Christian ministry to people on the move is relatively new and its significance and potential have still to be recognised by many churches and mission organisations. Comparatively few studies of this kind of ministry exist, and an even smaller number include relevant theological reflection. This chapter explores existing scholarship relevant to migration in East Asia.

Evangelical Writings on Migration

Missiology's 'Mission and Migration'

The American Society of Missiology devoted the January 2003 issue of their journal to migration, identifying two motifs from Christian scripture relevant to the East Asian context. The first is the obligation for God's people to show hospitality to the stranger, and the second is the status of the community of YHWH as strangers and aliens themselves.

In the issue, Christine Pohl contrasts institutionalised ideas of church today with the early church's attractive mixture of outreach, worship, and hospitality. In an age of fragmentation, people are looking to belong and thus Christians must form 'communities of hospitality' which manifest the kingdom. She rejects the traditional dichotomy of outreach (within one's own culture) and mission (across cultures and beyond borders), embracing an approach described as *missional.* This nuanced understanding of mission is especially relevant for ministry to migrants because it is cross-cultural even though done by ordinary Christians in the host community. Hospitality may speak volumes about belonging and faith to migrants who are separated from all that is familiar. However, even the offering of hospitality can become a power exercise in which hosts patronise the very guests they invite. When guests are allowed to take part in or take over meal preparation, conventional barriers are broken down and host Christians experience a 'theology of receiving'.

Another article comes from Samuel Escobar, a Peruvian urging the church in Europe to speak out against anti-migrant sentiment. He reminds the church of the 'ethical treasure that is part of the Western and European heritage' and which can defend the poor and the downtrodden, particularly the migrant. He provides a brief cameo in which a Bolivian lady in Germany shares the gospel with a Spanish immigrant through hospitality in her home, blurring distinctions between home and church and celebrating the empowering of the ordinary Christian as a missionary.

David Phillips' Nomad Theology

Theological educator and missionary David Phillips urges us to read the Bible through the eyes of travelling pastoral herders, as there are lessons for Christians as well as those they may try to reach. Nomadic peoples' inherent vulnerability means they attach importance to relationships rather than to material things and prioritise needs over desires. For the nomad, life is a journey to be experienced and a process as well as a goal, a basic orientation which resonates with the simple lifestyle and modest expectations of the foreign worker in East Asia.

Phillips looks at the OT patriarchs as nomads and describes Israel as 'permanent spiritual nomads' following a God who did not belong to any specific location or people. In the NT Peter refers to 'aliens and strangers' in his first letter, and Jesus' itinerant lifestyle, dynamic trust in his Father, and lack of material possessions could speak to Christians and migrants.

Ecumenical Writings on Migration

In a wide-ranging examination of migration in Europe, a report by the World Council Churches' Commission for Migrants, we read, 'There are friends and enemies, and there are strangers'. Strangers disturb the neat separation into insider and outsider, or between friend and foe. Also, most migrants' jobs mean that they may be seen and not heard and even provide services almost magically, without inclusion or even humanity.

Migration connects with all of the major themes of the Bible and runs through the scripture like a 'red thread'. The experience of the alien in Israel offers revealing insights into the manner in which God expected his people to relate to the outsider (the 'Other'), an obligation which persists into the New Testament period and remains valid for the church today.

God's relationship with the stranger is central to the biblical story, as he meets his people when they faced servitude, humiliation, and shame. Justice for the alien is part of the logic of the God of the poor and our treatment of the alien must be informed by the Exodus event. The Exodus memory is not only for Jews, and should inform the self-understanding of Christians.

We who are called to become strangers in the NT are reminded that there should no longer be any strangers among us. Galatians 3 and Ephesians 2 emphasise equality and reconciliation and reject discrimination. Our convictions about the value of the individual are drawn directly from the creation story and we must not withhold the gift of grace from those created in God's image.

The Hebrew insistence on the rights of the alien is a consequence of God's desire that people enjoy *shalom* in a world marred by both societal and individual sin. Martin Luther speaks of *homo incurvatus in se ipsum* ('man curved in on himself'), connecting our separation from God and each other, and later theologians warn of *communio incurvata in se ipsam* ('a community curved in upon itself'). Rather than simply accepting the inward turning which results from sin we are to seek the higher ground and define ourselves by the reality of love.

For Jesus and James (in the second half of James 2) the locking together of faith and ethics means that the community of YHWH faith should curve outward. An 'ethics of empathy' means that we should feel *for* the Other because we have felt *like* the Other.

Roman Catholic Perspectives

The Roman Catholic Church has been concerned for migrants for a long time, from the first official statements in 1914 to the Vatican's *Exsul Familia* in 1952, which became the *Magna Carta* of the Church's teaching on migration. It begins with the escape of Jesus and his parents to Egypt and takes this as the reason that the Holy Family can identify with migrants. More recently, the 2004 *Erga migrantes caritas Christi* (The love of Christ towards migrants) demonstrates the church's concern for migrants, although the redemptive message of the gospel is harder to find.

Asian Catholic Viewpoints from 'Faith on the Move'

Faith on the Move: Toward a Theology of Migration in Asia is a compilation of conference papers and arguably the first theologically informed treatment of migration in East Asia by any part of the church. It discusses the responsibility of Christians to others and reminds us that early church fathers such as Clement of Rome, John Chrysostom, and Ambrose of Milan all mention the Christian duty of hospitality. This theme of welcoming the Other is extremely significant.

American scholar Daniel Groody, who worked among Mexican migrants, proposed four fundamentals of a theology of migration: *imago Dei*, *verbum Dei*, *missio Dei*, and *visio Dei*, each of which requires Christians to break through human barriers. Beginning with the image of God, Groody first objects to labels such as 'migrant' or 'refugee' because they emphasise 'political status rather than... human identity'. He opposes the dehumanising effect of labels and contrasts 'inner identity' with 'imposed external identity'.

The concept of the *imago Dei* asks how much a country's economy contributes to the dignity of human beings, particularly the marginalised. The incarnation of Christ as *verbum Dei* suggests an openness to the Father and a willingness to speak with humanity which should mark our lives too. Groody reminds us that whereas human migration seeks improvement, divine migration moves downwards. He paraphrases Karl Barth: Christ's journey is not away from, but towards 'alienation, difference, and otherness' and is an offence to our sinful human values and categories. Willingness to engage the Other must affect our relationships with people both inside and outside the church and is derived from a God who is not afraid of 'downward mobility'. After all, this movement of God to us makes possible our movement to him. Christ's migration is part of the *missio Dei*, which encompasses every aspect of every person as Christians challenge borders and engage in reconciliation. Our attitudes and actions in the here and now must be determined by our heavenly citizenship and the church must connect with people on the 'wrong side of the lines'.

Orthodoxy: Zizioulas 'Communion and Otherness'

The Eastern Orthodox theologian Zizioulas explores the problem of the Other in the locus of western culture. He is worth quoting at length:

> *In our culture protection from the other is a fundamental necessity. We feel more and more threatened by the presence of the other. We are forced and even encouraged to consider the other as our enemy before we can treat him*

> *or her as our friend. Communion with the other is not spontaneous; it is built upon fences which protect us from the dangers implicit in the other's presence. We accept the other only in so far as he or she does not threaten our privacy or in so far as he or she is useful for our individual happiness.*

These words arise from his observation of western societies yet are relevant to other contexts.

To promote recognition and acceptance of the Other, Zizioulas introduces *difference* and *division*. Difference is the healthy acknowledgement of Otherness while division is negative and isolating. Drawing on the rich Trinitarian heritage of his church tradition, he describes the Otherness that exists between the members of the Trinity as an essential condition for their unity. This is a healthy otherness of *difference* accepted, rather than an otherness in which unity exists in spite of and in the face of *division*.

Two Modern Jewish Philosophers: Buber and Levinas

Martin Buber and Emmanuel Levinas were two Jewish philosophers separated by World War Two and their adopted homelands. Buber was a German Jew writing before the war, while the Lithuanian Levinas took up residence in Paris and wrote in the light of the Holocaust.

In his classic *I and Thou* Buber lays out a framework for relationships between people, in which he argues that *I* can never exist alone. He classifies relationships into two types: the *I-thou* and the *I-it*. In one case, we *speak* to a person and look him or her in the eye, while in the other we *refer* to a person or entity almost obliquely. The *I-thou* relation involves the whole person and recognises their humanity whereas the *I-it* does not. The unique relationship between God and people is called *I-eternal Thou*.

Exploitation or commodification of female domestic helpers is not unknown in Christian circles; thus a Christian may pray to God in an *I-eternal Thou* relationship but persist in exploitative, utilitarian practices which downgrade a migrant *thou* to an *it*. Loving God with our whole being emphasises the relationship between *I* and the *eternal Thou* and the commandment to love one's neighbour as oneself entails relating to *each and every* Other as *thou* and never as *it*.

Finally, Buber views community as a circle. True community (a perfect circle) can only exist when all the *I*'s are joined to the Centre (the *eternal Thou*) by radii of equal length such that all members are of equal significance.

By contrast, much of Levinas' work is based on consideration of the Other as 'what I am not', and emerges from his reflections on the Holocaust. Although the Other is defined in terms of *non-I*, for Levinas we must choose to view him or her as 'someone who could be kin' rather than a threat. The presence of another person, a human 'face' in front of us, brings an ethical demand and responsibility.

Miroslav Volf's 'Exclusion and Embrace'

Croatian theologian Miroslav Volf writes against the background of ethnic strife in the former Yugoslavia. He considers the importance of the recognition we receive from those around us and urges us to pay attention to the kind of people we are in order to promote harmonious relationships with others. Theologians should shape people into those who bring about truth and justice to societies, both individually and nationally. This is of particular relevance for East Asia, where abuse of migrants is sometimes justified by reference to unjust legal frameworks. He reminds us that Christians so often identify with the mainstream culture that they are unable or unwilling to stand against it. There will always be victims of muggings on the road between Jerusalem and Jericho, but if we go and help, there will be one less lying there.

Liminality and Communitas

In modern scholarship, liminality is a term applied to those in transition, who are neither one thing nor the other and who function as outsiders. The term is derived from the Latin word *limen*, meaning a *threshold*, and refers to the notion of 'in between-ness'. Communitas is the bond between strangers or pilgrims thrown together by liminal circumstances offering excitement but also intimacy. It is the social milieu created when people interact in the liminal situation, spontaneously, freely, and liberated from externally imposed and recognised social norms.

A Thai construction worker on a fixed contract in Taiwan may experience a semi-permanent liminal state in which his sense of belonging or acceptance is virtually zero and has no potential to change while he is in the country. On the other hand, a Filipina domestic helper may remain with the same Singapore family for years and build strong relationships with its members, particularly children who grow up partially under her care. Thus, a broad and flexible concept of liminality is applied to the realities of migration in East Asia.

Liminality and communitas can also bring liberation from old structures and modes of thought and openness to the new and exciting. However, the liberation brought by this liminal, 'betwixt and between' status should be enjoyed by the comfortable host as well as the vulnerable migrant.

A biblically and theologically robust response to migration in East Asia needs to draw on the wisdom of various parts of the church and our Jewish friends. Otherness, liminality, and communitas are significant new lenses through which to view the Bible for this purpose.

Migration and the Ancient Faith Community

Introduction

The primary aim of this chapter is to look at the injunctions relating to the alien which were given to Israel by God in the Pentateuch, which I call the 'alien mandate'.

The distinction between those who belong to the host community of faith and 'the Other' is fundamental to this treatment of migration. And it may be convenient to consider a triangular model which bears some similarity to Chris Wright's representation (see fig 1) of covenant promises. Wright shows how promises beginning with God are first manifest through the people of Israel and then expanded to the church. Then, to represent the new covenant, he adds a larger triangle with the same apex, as God is the origin of promises under both covenants. In this larger triangle, the whole of mankind is at the bottom left (an expanded form of the people of Israel) and the whole earth at the bottom right, an extension of the physical land of Israel.

I propose a second, analogous triangular model for thinking about the alien. God is at the top of the triangle of the faith community because it originally grew from him and at the moment of creation it was a singularity: God and God alone. Later, under the old covenant, Israel projects out from him, reaching out into the world but distinct from it. Later still, extending further outwards from Israel is the new community of faith since the coming of Christ (see fig 2).

If the triangles represent the growing community of faith then the space around them represents people outside it. For the current research the boundaries of the triangles are significant as interfaces between *faith and no-faith* or *faith and other-faith*. At these interfaces, transmission of faith and implementation of biblical social concern and justice can occur. These regions are spaces of Otherness and liminality for both faith bearer and faith recipient.

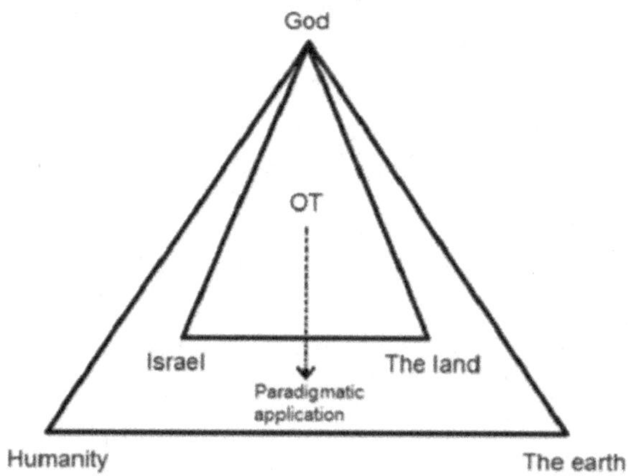

Fig 1. Wright's paradigmatic relationship between the covenants.

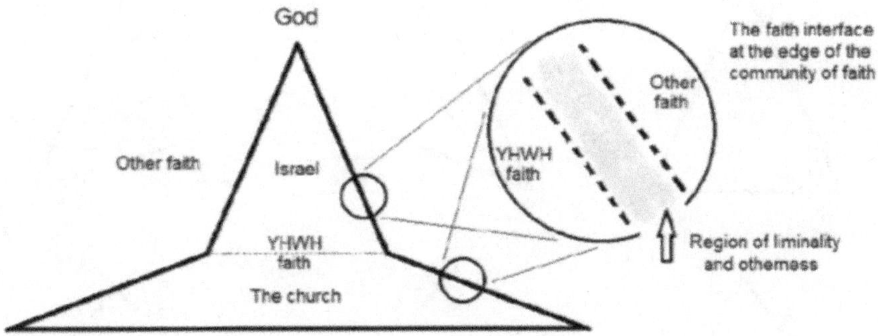

Fig 2. The expanding community and the faith interface.

In both Testaments, the attitude of the community of YHWH faith (those who believe in the God of the Bible in both Testaments) to the Other involves the two related factors of spiritual dependence on God and the social justice which such faith entails. This missional triangle has God at the apex and spiritual redemption at one lower corner and social justice at the other (see fig 3, overleaf). Both lower corners are important and as mission proceeds should move outwards at the same rate to promote integrated, biblical shalom.

God

The beginning of the Bible proclaims that God is distinct from that which he created but desires community between himself and his people, because he is a community within himself. God has always been Trinitarian, even if that was not clearly revealed in the Old

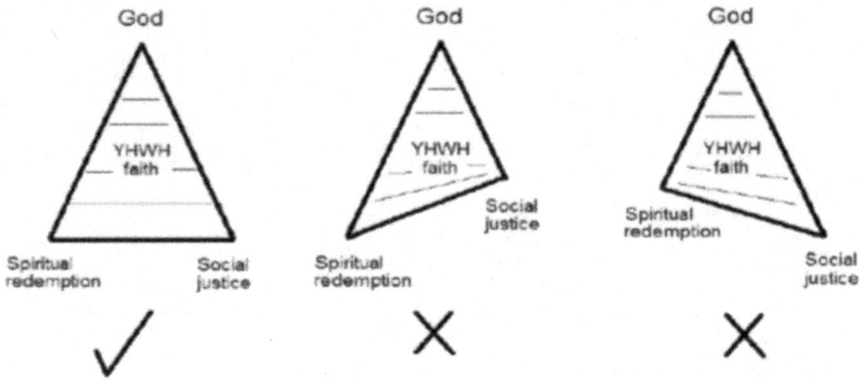

Fig 3. The balance between spiritual redemption and social justice.

Testament! With the creation of the first man and first woman, the faith community grows from a divine singularity to a triangle, albeit a very small one. Adam and Eve are dependent on God for life, both spiritual and physical, and his care for them even after the Fall reflects the two corners of the missional triangle. After the Fall, God's interaction with Israel continues to be liminal, the overlap of the 'divine and human realms'. The scriptures suggest that the liminal experiences are different for God and Israel, as one party is infinite, loving, and sinless, while the other is finite, fickle, and sinful.

God's people rejected him religiously, morally, socially, and politically, which brought about complete alienation between the two parties. God's pain as Other is portrayed very poignantly in Hosea 11. His statement of love for Israel in v.1 is followed by a lament in v.2: *The more I called Israel, the further they went from me*. God is no stranger to estrangement and negative Otherness.

Three Old Testament Aliens: Abraham, Joseph, and Moses

Abraham, Joseph, and Moses are spiritual ancestors for Jew and Christian alike. Abraham as father of the nation and exemplar of faith became an alien in obedience to God and that has implications for those who claim to be his spiritual descendants. Joseph is likewise a hero of faith and saviour of the nation during famine. Moses is the human architect of the Exodus and the recipient of the Law at Sinai. All three spent time in foreign countries and lived lives marked by Otherness and liminality.

Abraham

Abraham is asked to leave his country, people, and father's household for an unknown destination, breaking ties with his familial and cultural community. He is to throw himself on the mercy of God as he inaugurates a new community of faith and experience Otherness and liminality which would ultimately benefit those who would come after him.

He also makes provision for the inclusion of foreigners who might not immediately acknowledge the God of the covenant. Here is early evidence of a tension between religious and social belonging. This is central to any theology of migration in East Asia: how do Christians in the broader host society relate to religious, ethnic, and status Others (outsiders) who live in that society?

Joseph

Joseph's life as Other (an outsider?) begins while he is still at home, as his father's bias towards him has already caused a marginalisation which became more serious after Joseph's grandiose dreams about his future status. Marginalisation becomes expulsion when his brothers sell him to a group of Ishmaelites who take him to Egypt. As a slave in a foreign land, his life is marked by on-going coerced liminality.

Vulnerable and marginalised after false accusations by Potiphar's wife, he is thrown into jail, apparently without trial. His powerlessness at the mercy of the host community mirrors the experience of contemporary migrants.

After successfully interpreting the dreams of his fellow prisoners, Pharaoh's cupbearer and baker, Joseph is later called to provide the same service for Pharaoh himself. He is a foreigner, but works at the centre of government; he was a slave but is now the most powerful man in the land; he has faith in YHWH, but his father-in-law is an Egyptian priest. Apparently, it is the right of the powerful to decide what types of Otherness to ignore and how much inclusion to practise.

Moses

By the time of Exodus, the coming of a new pharaoh has caused Israel to move from the status of near Other to toxic Other in the mind of the Egyptians. The adult Moses is 'betwixt and between'. In Exodus 2 he feels Hebrew enough to be outraged at seeing an Egyptian beating a Hebrew slave, but his feeling of identity is not shared by a Hebrew who saw him kill the Egyptian. In addition, he is a prince while those around him are slaves. His alienation is two-fold, by race and by class. After Moses flees to Midian and marries a non-Hebrew woman, his first son is called Gershom, the Hebrew root *ger* signifying Moses' status as an alien. His life ends in liminality, as he is not able to enter the Promised Land and dies betwixt and between.

Abraham, Moses, and Joseph are heroic figures in Jewish history and their time as migrants is a vital part of their identities. Their stories contain important lessons about Otherness and liminality and the migrant experience under the protection of God. As examples for Jew and Christian alike it is noteworthy that their faith under such conditions is praised in Hebrews 11. The stories of the nation of Israel and its heroic figures suggest that Otherness and liminality are normative for YHWH and those who follow him.

The Mission of Israel: Being before Going?

The church's relative uncertainty about whether ministry to migrants is mission can be addressed by considering a combination of centripetal and centrifugal approaches. From this point of view, it is helpful to look at the Old Testament view of mission, where Israel's main responsibility was *to be* rather than *to go*. Going (centrifugal) is not ruled out, but at that time in salvation-history the primary mode was centripetal.

Who is the Alien?

Three words are used to refer to foreigners in the Hebrew scriptures: *ger*, *toshab*, and *nekar*. Among these, *ger* is the most important and most common. The *ger* is a foreigner or alien (the term used in the NIV) who lives within the nation of Israel, '*the sojourner* or *the stranger who sojourns* among you' (King James). *Nekar* is a foreigner or outsider, *toshab* a hired worker.

The *ger* lives inside the nation of Israel for an extended period and is dependent upon a sponsor or employer of some kind. Originally the *ger* would have been attached to a household, the basic unit of production in an agricultural society. In the eyes of God, Israel has a solemn responsibility to act ethically and missionally towards the alien.

God's injunction to Israel is for the care of the alien, and to some extent this open-heartedness is evident in ancient Israel. Israel is commanded to extend the Sabbath rest to the alien, and in the Holiness Code commands concerning the alien often mention other vulnerable members of the community, such as widows and orphans. The sense is of social justice for all irrespective of Otherness. Other verses require land-owning Israelites to provide for the vulnerable, and whether it is leaving the corners of the field unreaped or allowing olives and grapes to remain on the trees and vines, the alien, widow, and orphan are to be provided for.

An alien wishing to celebrate the Passover had to be circumcised and then could take part as if native-born. Circumcision is important for the alien as it is the means by which he joins himself to the community of faith physically and spiritually. He is accepting God's provision and relying on God for something which he could not do for himself.

Three well-known Gentile believers feature in the Old Testament. We know from the sketchy account of Rahab the Gentile prostitute that although she exhibits the dual Otherness of race and status, she clearly placed her faith in YHWH and pledged her allegiance to his people. She appears in the genealogy of Jesus in Matthew 1:5 and is commended twice in the New Testament for living out her faith.

The story of Ruth is the most complete account of the integration of an alien into Israel. The daughter-in-law of an Israelite couple decides to follow her mother-in-law Naomi on her journey back to Israel after the death of the older lady's husband and two sons, one of whom was Ruth's husband. It is noteworthy that the original pledge of loyalty happens in Moab as Ruth commits to the Israelite family – this is centripetal mission, into a community, happening 'on the field', so to speak.

The story is complicated by Boaz' position as kinsman-redeemer and ultimately distorted by his romantic interest in Ruth! Nonetheless, the account of Ruth shows the Otherness and liminality of the alien with regard to the Israelite, first outside and then within Israel.

Naaman is a special case as he benefitted from God's mercy and expressed faith in him but did not remain in the community. His gratitude was genuine and he wanted to offer gifts to Elisha, and such was his faith that he took Israelite soil back home with him so that he could kneel in worship to YHWH. He overcame ethnic differences and his own pride to submit himself to the Israelites and their God, and Jesus praises his faith in Luke's gospel.

God is the source of blessing and positive Otherness, and these factors are meant to cascade down from him to Israel and thence on to the alien, which has direct and paradigmatic relevance for the church in East Asia today.

Migration and the Expanding Faith Community

Jesus the Other

Jesus' life and experience on earth are marked by multiple Othernesses, and Matthew traces his roots through Joseph to Abraham the wandering alien and bearer of the multi-ethnic promise and commission of God in Genesis 12. In a gospel written for Jewish readers, the blood of three Gentile women, Rahab a prostitute, Ruth a poor migrant, and Bathsheba an adulteress, flows in his veins.

The Magi in Matthew and the Shepherds in Luke

The infant Christ is visited by scholars of astronomy and astrology from Central Asia or perhaps Babylon. We know little about them, but we do know that these Gentiles present the new-born king with gifts as an act of worship. Like Naaman, they enter the Jewish community of faith temporarily and acknowledge the King of the Jews as theirs. God's provision of the guiding star and the warning to them in a dream are proof of his hand in and approval of the inclusion of aliens.

Luke's shepherds are the exact opposite, for although Jewish, they were marginalised and did 3D jobs – difficult, dirty, and dangerous. The presence of these two different groups is an affirmation of the Other, whether racial outsider or social outcast.

Jesus' Early Life

Jesus' birth is marked by Otherness and liminality. The unmarried Mary is informed of her pregnancy by an angel, and Joseph is discouraged from divorcing her in a dream. Jesus was born in a stable to parents displaced by the census of a foreign power and later taken to Egypt to escape the murderous intentions of Herod before returning to Israel.

Thus at the incarnation God migrated in Christ, and Jesus pitches his migrant tent among us, exposing himself to marginalisation and rejection at the hands of those he had created. These continued through his life and in his death, in a spiritual agony beyond the understanding of his creatures Jesus cries out, 'My God, my God, why have You forsaken me?' These words suggest a state of toxic Otherness, as he 'experienced full alienation from God'.

Relevant Teaching in the Gospels

Much of Jesus' teaching is relevant to migration in East Asia, and the parables of the mustard seed and the yeast demonstrate that the kingdom will grow from small beginnings but eventually contain many people. Together they represent juxtapositions of great and small, purity and impurity, and an 'overturning of conventions' such that the liminality of the kingdom would make sense to people who followed Jesus. I believe that a synthesis of the two parables in the context of migration points to advocacy on behalf of migrants undertaken by Christians in small and gentle ways.

If the kingdom of God is the continuation and expansion of God's rule in the Old Testament, pointing to and anticipating the full consummation of God's reign on earth, then logically the church has an obligation to do more than was required of the Israelites. This includes greater compassion for the Other and willingness to enter into liminal situations as well as a more outward facing and expansionist mentality. As the kingdom goes out, it must attract people in.

The well-known story of the Good Samaritan employs stereotypes of insider and outsider. The Samaritan, of whom nothing would be expected and to whom nothing would be given, moves himself into a liminal space as he crosses boundaries established by Jews. He is an outsider entering their world, yet he comes from a position of relative strength because circumstances have made the Jew the weaker party. Communitas emerges as the Samaritan gives first-aid to the victim and takes him to the inn. As the Samaritan undertakes to take care of any further expenses on his return, commitment and trust develop between him, the injured man, and the innkeeper.

The exchange comes to a climax with the definition of *neighbour* as one who meets the needs of others and enters liminal spaces by crossing established barriers. The story is directly relevant to migration and in it there are harsh warnings for the church. Insiders, religious, racial, and social failed in their duty, and the one who showed mercy and compassion was himself an outsider, an Other.

Jesus' final time with the whole group of disciples was in the Upper Room where he, the leader and teacher, washes his disciples' feet, to demonstrate that having the gospel and bringing it to others involves serving them. This brings an unwelcome disturbance of social order and accepted hierarchies.

Later, when the Risen Lord appeared on the shore, Peter must have felt vulnerable and marginal. Jesus acts to reduce his Otherness and reaffirm him as part of the group but insists that Peter's expressed love for him must manifest as care for the church. Jesus has acted radically to restore Peter after his denial and rescue him from a distant Otherness of his own making by accepting and affirming him.

Jesus Interacts with Individual Others

Jesus interacts with different kinds of Otherness in many of his dealings with people. One example is the case of the Samaritan woman, which forms a bridge between Jesus' dealings with Jews and with Gentiles. In his interaction with her, both Jesus and the woman are in a liminal space. He is a Jew and has entered Samaritan territory, usually avoided by Jews. She is at home but excluded from her natural in-group as shown by her presence at the well at noon. The two people are separated by race and religion, social status, and gender. Jesus bridges all of these barriers yet in so doing moves the 'semi-pagan peasant' Samaritan woman over to his side.

The fact that she is a Samaritan, a woman, and a person with a complex history does not prevent Jesus transmitting the message of redemption to her, which she subsequently shares with her people. The result is the taking of Messianic faith across boundaries and the bringing of Others into a community of faith whose racial and theological roots were Jewish.

Jesus combines loving inclusiveness with an insistence that faith in God is essential, echoing the inclusive-exclusive tension of the Old Testament and anticipating the teaching of the epistles. It was Jesus' secure relationship of Otherness with his Father and self-giving love for fallen humanity that caused Jesus to enter the liminal space in the first place. Liminality is the result of a choice made at the incarnation.

Other contacts between Jesus and Gentiles are illustrative of a transition to a broader and more inclusive understanding of the YHWH faith community including the centurion of Luke 7, the Syro-Phoenician woman of Matthew 15 (arguing that a person of lower ethno-religious status can be part of the faith community) and the Samaritan Leper of Luke 17 (who was the only one who returned to give thanks). Foreigners migrating into the community of faith are told by Christ, 'Your faith has made you well', which speaks of a general state of wholeness and well-being.

These three brief accounts show non-Jews exercising faith across boundaries, and migrating into the community of faith by trusting Jesus. His status as the God-man means that he links together Creator and created, and Israel and the Gentile-including kingdom. He draws from his perfect relationship of Otherness with his Father to model and empower the church to manage Otherness well and attract outsiders into the kingdom, at the heart of which is the Trinity itself.

In the Book of Acts we see how the early church responded to Gentiles and brought them into a Jewish community of Christian faith, and a comprehensive review of the remaining books of the New Testament (to be found in the original thesis) points to the fact that the church inherits the liminal status of ancient Israel. The kingdom community draws its life from the Triune God and generates an attractive vector towards the outside world. The love of God and his own perfect management of Otherness within the Godhead are brought to the followers of Christ as a community by the incarnate Son. The cross means that all human distinctions of race, status, and gender are not extinguished but become meaningless for salvation. At the same time, the only category which preserves any meaning is whether or not a person has faith in God through Christ. The result should be a community of faith which takes from God and models it to the surrounding world, by its witness and kindness attracting people to join. This modelling of healthy Otherness and reconciliation between races and social groups is relevant for ministry by hosts to migrants.

Towards a Response to Migration in East Asia

In the Old Testament period, (resident) aliens were Others (outsiders) on the periphery of mainstream Israelite society, separated from the host community of faith by race, social status, and ultimately, absence of faith in Israel's God. Israelite society was to be welcoming and just in its dealings with Gentile aliens, granting them a high degree of access to mainstream Israelite society, and even letting them take part in certain religious ceremonies. However, the access was limited; in order to enjoy all the benefits and privileges of the Israelites, the alien had to take a step of faith and pledge him or herself to their God through circumcision.

Through the life, work, and death of Christ, many Old Testament concepts are broadened and deepened, such that kingdom themes which applied to Israel are now expanded into the idea of 'God's people in God's place under God's rule'.

Certain aspects of God's nature, character, experience, and action, including care for the lost and disadvantaged, cascade down from him. The community of faith is to be a pipe rather than a bucket, to pass on good things from God to the world that he cares for. The church takes on this Otherness and liminality as a community which draws from God at its centre and shares life with those around it.

The purpose of mission is to manifest the Christian community and attract people to join; the *going out* is meant to facilitate the *coming in*, removing a false dichotomy between centripetal and centrifugal mission. The aim is to bring a redemptive message and practice which invites people to become part of the local incarnation of a new humanity, in which toxic Otherness is transformed into healthy acceptance. It is of no consequence whether cross-cultural mission takes place in the country of the target people or in the home nation of the so-called missionary; gospel ministry among migrants is true cross-cultural mission.

The discussion of Otherness and differential liminality of host and migrant has implications for Christians from a Confucian heritage who live in a region where some national immigration policies tolerate the exploitation of migrants. This is not to single out Confucianism, it is simply a consequence of reflecting theologically on sociological phenomena in this region. Migration literature also details exploitation and unfair treatment in Europe and North America.

However, the fusion of traditional attitudes to race among Chinese, Japanese, and Korean people with Confucian familism and the notion of the country as extended family have resulted in some exclusivist and dismissive attitudes to foreigners in the three cultures, particularly those of darker skin colour or from poorer countries. Also, Confucian notions of hierarchy tend to work against those in lower status or service jobs. Many migrants in Asia experience a toxic nexus of racial and status attitudes locked into a rigid and exclusivist framework of belonging.

The Bible cuts across all of this, redefining attitudes to race and status. That the Bible presents God's people as Other and liminal is also a challenge to the host Christian. The message is uncompromising: Christians are to go the extra mile and reach out to those around them. The fact that the host is settled and comfortable and the migrant unstable and vulnerable merely strengthens the responsibility of the former to act in a Christ-like way. The host is commanded to enter the liminal space with the migrant, and Phillips asks us to see ourselves as nomads.

There seems to be a disconnect between the recent national heritage of Christians in the region and their relative slowness to adopt biblical principles derived from the analogous experience of the Israelites, The corporate memory of Israel in Egypt advocates fair treatment of aliens, and the six Asian territories have each had their own Egypt experience of colonisation, displacement, or occupation by foreign powers. Many citizens' forefathers migrated from foreign countries and within living memory there are stories of struggle, discrimination, vulnerability, and exploitation. One of the central features of Singapore's 2011 National Day Parade was a theatrical re-enactment of the arrival by boat of thousands of Chinese and Indian immigrants, with performers dressed in old-fashioned ethnic costumes carrying suitcases and boxes splashing through shallow water. Yet recently there was a mild furore at a government plan to locate a foreign workers' hostel near a residential neighbourhood, with much talk in the media about the undesirability and danger of foreign labourers. Eventually the government located the hostel far away from residential areas.

However, scripture requires Christians in the region to look back to their spiritual heritage in the Exodus and the future promise of the second Exodus in Christ and embrace their own Otherness and liminality. Followers of Christ have a biblical mandate to be countercultural and transformational, humbly but biblically dissatisfied with the *status quo*.

Anchoring a Response to Migration within Existing Scholarship

At this point it is appropriate to pause and anchor these principles for a theological and missiological response to migration within broader scholarship. This is because this study of the Old and New Testament scriptures from the dual perspectives of Otherness and liminality marks a departure from previous theological reflection on migration.

Moltmann's Theology of Hope

Moltmann's view is that the church has the responsibility of bringing humanity and society into a future eschatological consummation of justice and righteousness. The eschatological hope points us forward but cannot remain future only; it must move the church to present action, proclamation and transformation going hand in hand. He argues for a kingdom mindset which changes not only individuals but also relationships and institutions.

Schluter and Ashcroft's 'Jubilee Manifesto'

The *Jubilee Manifesto* is a large and complex work promoting a relational approach to faith in society. A person's identity and sense of belonging are inextricably bound up with relationships past and present. A migrant will have undergone rupture of some relationships and the formation of new ones with people in the transnational space. Certain policies and attitudes in the host nations make it difficult for outsiders to form relationships with local people, and their short stay may also make it difficult for them to form friendships with fellow travellers. Closeness to fellow migrants may remind people of closer and deeper relationships with those back home, which are now impoverished or even dysfunctional. Love, space, and service cascade down from within the Godhead to the incarnate Son, to the redeemed people of God in the church, and out into the world.

The cornerstone of Catholic Social Teaching is the dignity and social reality of the human being. All cultures, but especially those with strong group identities, well-defined group boundaries, and binary distinctions of race and class, have four possible combinations of the singular (*I, thou*) and plural (*we, you*) parties at the end of the relationship. In addition to the classic *I-thou* we must consider *I-you* and *we-thou* and *we-you.* That is to say, how do groups of hosts relate to groups of migrants, and how do single individuals interact with groups? Further, what kind of groups are relevant in the migration context? Finally, where policy and cultural attitudes create a power dynamic biased in favour of the host society, the *we* element to the left of the dash is significant.

Shalom has its origin in God and works for the benefit of people, but always in community. Christians cannot enjoy shalom while denying it to Others around them. Negatively, shalom is the opposite of selfishness, division and hostility and its absence brings inequality and exclusive attitudes. Unless we are in communities that are caring and inclusive, a true understanding of shalom remains elusive. Shalom means that the church has to take risks and be serious about its prophetic role. Individual piety and action are not enough.

Liberation Theology

As a theological movement focused on the emancipation of the poor and disadvantaged, liberation theology has relevance for migration in East Asia, although the socio-political contexts and systems of this region are different from those in Latin America.

Liberation theologians argue that personal concern for the poor is not enough and Christians must also critique systems which perpetuate poverty. However, where liberation theology talks about radically changing the social system, the political and economic realities of the six territories and the surrounding home countries of migrants suggest something more modest, and indeed the kingdom parables of Matthew 13 advocate a bottom-up approach. Transformation should begin with attitudes and behaviour in the home and the church, and any public advocacy in the civil society must be gentle and winsome. Indeed, the liberation of the oppressed would restore the credibility which the gospel had in the early church. A response to migration in East Asia could benefit from a theology derived from a totally different context and has lessons to learn from the liberation theology movement in South America.

Catholic Social Teaching

Some Catholic theologians have linked Catholic social teaching and biblical notions of social justice, joining the dignity of human beings with compassion and justice for the poor, to result in acts of charity and efforts to change social structures. The recognition that the root of human dignity is the *imago Dei* should result in the reduction of Otherness.

The guiding principles of CST, drawn from summaries of the Vatican's vast *Compendium of the Social Doctrine of the Church* (2004), list six main principles. The first is human dignity. Because we bear God's image, respect is due to all regardless of race or status and cannot be lost; the *eternal Thou* stands behind every person. Next comes solidarity: Levinas' idea of the *face* brings an ethical appeal to love our neighbours as ourselves. The third idea, the common good, concerns all flourishing together with no one left behind. These three principles require Christians to look beyond themselves. The fourth concept is the universal destination of goods. What God has created is for everyone, and resources should be used appropriately. Under the fifth principle, participation, people have the right and responsibility to be part of decisions affecting them. The sixth principle is subsidiarity, empowerment of the grassroots and protection from imposed policies. To these are added advocacy for the poor and weak, and the encouragement to celebrate diversity in unity and live as social beings by analogy with the Trinity.

The two Catholic perspectives, liberation theology and Catholic social teaching provide a similar fusion of compassion and justice, applied into specific situations. Together they could inspire the church as it responds to migration in East Asia.

Towards a Theological Response

While the history and traditional practices of mission have been dominated by the centrifugal, outward movement of missionaries to unbelieving societies, this does not invalidate centripetal, inward attraction of unbelieving people to Christian communities. Ministry to migrants means that it is now unbelievers rather than missionaries who are on the move, and the direction of movement is into societies with established churches rather than out to so-called non-Christian lands.

The Confucian worldview espouses strong group identity and hierarchical attitudes. Family is a central idea, and companies and even nation-states are understood as expansions of it. A tightly-knit, interdependent community with strong leadership and a sense of history relating back to the ancestors requires loyalty from and provides support to its members. However, this inward focus may mean that those outside the family are effectively beyond any boundaries of care or respect, unless there is an existing relationship of some kind. Further, the emphasis on and preservation of social status means that those at the lower end of the social economic scale and those who perform menial or 3D tasks are treated with less respect than those higher up the ladder. The Other is truly an outsider.

The Confucian family has well-defined boundaries which are porous enough to allow new members to join, by marriage for example. Biblical teaching affirms Confucian concepts of the family but expands their scope, describing Christians as brothers (and sisters) regardless of blood ties, race, and status. Family persists, but the multiple cascadings from the Godhead to the community of faith mean its care now extends to those who do and might belong to Christ.

This broader understanding provides a framework in which members of other races can cross the boundary and become part of the family of Christian faith in Confucian cultures. This does not deny racial differences, but makes them irrelevant to the question of salvation and belonging. Indeed, the spirit of the scriptures requires that we are to glory in and celebrate the diversity found inside the family.

If Christians from a Confucian heritage bring these biblical principles into their idea of family and belonging, then Otherness is reduced and a new communitas results, a redemptive communitas of hosts stepping into the liminal space with migrants and treating them with respect and love as family members *in potentia*. This would be a new way for Christians in the host community to deal with migrant people, many of whom are to all intents and purposes invisible.

If Christians are to be salt and light then the educational process has to begin inside the church, changing attitudes one family at a time, including children. In countries where children routinely encounter domestic helpers and migrant workers it is necessary that their Christian identity includes healthy attitudes to Others.

Related to this is advocacy, and liberation theology encourages Christians to challenge attitudes and systems which oppress. Many churches in East Asia have large numbers of white-collar members with influence in business, civil service, and even government circles, who can bring biblical attitudes to the Other into real life situations. In East Asia, liberation theology requires Christians not to liberate and empower themselves but to grant Exodus to migrant Others in their midst. Likewise, Catholic social teaching asks Christians to look to the common good and to take care of the weak because all are created in God's image. In addition, it suggests a process of observation, assessment, and response. Christians in East Asia could open their eyes to the exploitation and oppression that goes on around them, not in far-off countries but in their own neighbourhoods and in some cases their own houses, and then make assessments according to biblical principles, which would then lead them to respond in action of one kind or another.

If they are willing to enter the liminal spaces with migrants, Christians in the host country can learn to extend acceptance and material generosity to them. Many migrants come from relatively poor countries in East Asia and a domestic helper in Singapore may be paid around S$300 per month, around one eighth of the salary of a fresh graduate in the country. It may be difficult to imagine contract labourers or domestic helpers having Christian fellowship with professionals and business people, but the example is Christ and his establishment of new communities through table fellowship. Such can be expected in the communitas created by the gospel, and healthy relationships and Otherness may reduce some of the tensions created by income differentials and even encourage employers to pay their domestic helpers or contract labourers more and look to empower them and develop their potential.

Towards a Missiological Response

Whether ministry to migrants occurs in the host country or in the home country, it will involve the extension of the kingdom of God and a space of acceptance from the church and out into a group of people who are quite different from the mainstream host society. Multiple interfaces will be established, across which faith can be transferred from host to migrant, across gulfs of language and culture, as well as race and status.

Response of Host Nation Churches to Migrants in the Host Nations

Many migrants in East Asia come from countries where the church cannot minister freely or where there could be consequences for those who become Christians. Socialist countries like China and Vietnam outlaw unregistered churches and place restrictions on government-approved church bodies. Indonesia and Thailand do have religious freedom but local religions such as Islam or Buddhism are strong and it can be challenging for a person to return as a Christian.

Ethnic fellowships already exist in the six countries, for example groups of Filipinos or Indonesians meeting on the premises of local churches. The host churches may defray some of their expenses, send people to help out with logistics, and even employ ethnic pastors to run them. In what I call remote access or remote control ministry, a committed church in Seoul may support a Mongolian fellowship, and a mainly Chinese church in Singapore may sponsor a meeting for Indonesian domestic helpers. But this state of affairs maintains a silo effect in which the two groups have practically no interaction with each other. The gospel is proclaimed and lives are changed, but distant Otherness remains, and these meetings are not even multicultural, let alone intercultural. In a rather detached way, the host community meets the needs of a group of migrants or perhaps their own perception of those needs, but in a way which requires no transformation of the hosts.

A number of Singapore churches now work among Mainland Chinese labourers, laying on coaches to bring large numbers of them to the church for a gospel programme, a simple meal, and sometimes some training in English or learning the guitar. However, the underlying assumption is that what works for Singaporeans will help lonely men who are far from home and have no idea about the Christian message. The felt needs of contract workers from China and primarily middle-class Singaporeans are very different, suggesting that ministry by local churches may need to be precisely targeted and contextualised.

These factors highlight a fundamental issue for those reaching migrants. Because most will be in the host country for a limited period and they are different from local people, migrants often remain in a state of village transnationalism, in which co-ethnic labour and cultural presence extend aspects of the village in the home country into the host nation. The implication is that what might be criticised as a detached or simplistic approach may seem to be the best option, and so dedicated ethnic fellowships seem to be at least partly justified.

However, this does not address the question of Otherness and the reconciliation brought by the gospel. Nor does it bring about changes in attitude in migrants or host Christians. Another problem would be the lack of mature Christian role models from whom migrants could learn about the influence of Christianity on the individual, marriage and family, business and so on. Also, many domestic helpers do speak English and spend time in close contact with local people, and, depending on their jobs, contract workers may also gain fluency in the local *lingua franca*. The same is true for students and foreign brides.

Ministry to migrants in the host countries needs to take account of their identity in the transnational space, in a state of village transnationalism, while at the same time trying to reduce Otherness with regard to Christians in the host community. Also, the resources in the host community can be used to benefit migrants. Village transnationalism transfers and to some extent preserves, for example, life in rural Thailand within the urban environment of Singapore, and thus ministry needs considerable understanding of the circumstances and challenges of migrants' home situations.

Models of ministry to migrants in the West have often assumed settlement or gradual acculturation, either to the mainstream host society or ethnic diaspora communities in that society, but the distinctive feature of migration in East Asia is that it is usually time-limited, with migrants returning home after a few years.

Transnational spaces and migration systems that link migrants at home with specific opportunities in particular sectors of industries or companies in host societies, result in a particular set of circumstances for Christian work among them. Migrants may come to the host countries with little knowledge or interest in the gospel, yet if exposed to the Christian message may take some knowledge of it back to their home communities. If a migrant does come to faith then he or she needs to survive as a Christian in a possibly unwelcoming or even hostile environment back home. Those who make good progress in their faith could theoretically constitute a low-key and culturally savvy missionary force to their own home countries, requiring neither visa nor culture or language training.

Migrants converted while abroad will become relatively Other to their original host societies. Their formative experience of the faith will have taken place in a foreign country, influenced to some extent by foreign and probably western Christianity. Thus, whether migrants expect to remain for the medium term or return home after a short contract, their Christian understanding and praxis must be relevant to the transnational space. If a Thai labourer becomes a Christian in Taiwan, then part of his Christian experience in that foreign country needs to prepare him for Christian life and witness in the transnational space in which he lives in Taiwan but also among fellow Thais in Thailand when he returns. The kindness of well-equipped local churches may help ethnic fellowships, but in order to maintain a flourishing and transformational Christian presence on their return migrant Christians need to be equipped to establish churches that are self-governing, self-propagating, and self-financing. We can also add the fourth self, self-theologising, because migrant fellowships in the transnational space need to be able to deal with issues facing returnees and the broader society in the home country.

Conclusions, Implications, and Suggestions

Although migration is a relatively new subject for theologians and missiologists to reflect upon, there are already resources in the church which can help shape its response to the phenomenon.

The review of the nature of migration suggested that in the Asian context there are fault lines between people of the host culture and incoming migrants, based on race, status, and gender. Government policies and attitudes of many in the host countries serve to create a rather utilitarian, *us-and-them* mentality between host and migrant. The gulf between the host and migrant has led to exploitation and abuse, and the church is knowingly or unknowingly part of this exploitative system. The primary implication is that race and status should lie at the heart of any theological reflection on migration.

The small amount of evangelical writing on migration originates in a context in which the assumption is that migrants will acculturate and settle, but this is not the case for most migrants in East Asia and there is considerable scope for further development of a theology of migration based on what has been written so far.

The contributions from ecumenical Protestants and Roman Catholics, together with the sociological study of migration, led to the identification of Otherness and liminality as two lenses with which to explore biblical content and theological ideas.

The Pentateuch contains the alien mandate, explicit instructions for how the Israelites were to relate to aliens residing in the community. The New Testament does not have these specific guidelines but gives broad principles for how the church should relate to racial and social Others.

Many churches and mission societies are beginning to minister to migrants, which has raised the question of whether such ministry is actually mission. For many who hold to a traditional home/field distinction, ministry among migrant people can fall through the cracks. Because such ministry happens in the same country as the church, it is often not considered as mission, and has lacked support and commitment. On the other hand, although the ministry happens at home, so to speak, it is truly cross-cultural and involves serving people with a variety of needs. For this reason, in the study of the Old and New Testament passages the concepts of centripetal and centrifugal mission were identified, especially as these relate to the early expansion of the church, by which Gentile believers effectively migrated into a Jewish church. The conclusion drawn is that ministry among migrant people is truly cross-cultural mission but combines centripetal and centrifugal approaches.

The Christian looks back to the deliverance from Egypt at the Exodus and forward to the final consummation of God's kingdom at the return of Christ. Because of their status as Other and liminal with regard to mainstream society, Christians can view themselves as fellow travellers with migrants.

The emphasis on fair treatment of aliens in the Old Testament and the requirements to treat one's neighbour as oneself in the New Testament come together to suggest that Christian believers should treat non-believers as believers: kindness, fair treatment, and acceptance are to be extended to them as is in line with the witness of the early church in Acts 2 and 4.

The theological ideas which emerged in this research could be used to extend very positive Confucian ideas of family and responsibility to all members or potential members of a Christian Confucian family based on the church.

Implications for a Missiological Response

The themes explored in this research suggest a continuum approach for ministry among migrants. Cultural and linguistic differences require that gospel ministry be contextualised for the migrants' situations and needs. Indonesians need to read the Bible in Bahasa Indonesia and many would approach it from an Islamic perspective. Vietnamese and Chinese would need to use their own languages and interact with Christians who understand ancestor worship, Confucianism, and socialist concepts of religion. Among mono-cultural groups of migrants, informal fellowships emphasising their culture and food may be very effective. However, because the migrants live in someone else's country and reconciliation and the reduction of Otherness lie at the centre of the gospel, meaningful exchange between migrants and host Christians is important. Therefore, some kind of church-based interaction between migrants and the host society seems desirable.

Local churches could hold occasional services in which locals and migrants worship together using songs from both cultures, simplified forms of the *lingua franca*, and/or interpretation. Short sharings and testimonies from both groups could be mutually encouraging and challenging as people meet in the liminal space. Alternatively, small groups of host Christians could visit ethnic fellowships. The details would vary a little, based on the background of the migrants and the profile of the church. However, the Bible gives host Christians the obligation to reach out and reduce Otherness.

Centripetal mission and the biblical requirement to reduce Otherness as a prelude to and result of conversion to Christ suggest that host Christians get involved in ethnic fellowships. However, local Christians may be used to highly organised and well-timed worship and may need to avoid the temptation to take over or make things 'more efficient'. As people of higher status and income, for them to show a genuine servant spirit towards the migrants would do much for the credibility of the gospel. Genuine worship with migrant Others would build relationships with God and between people of different race and status.

The affirmation of migrant Others could promote advocacy and practical help for them while reducing the tendency to ignore or treat them as a commodity. Local Christians could begin to see them as people with their own stories, needs, and aspirations, and it would be difficult to remain indifferent to the plight of migrants when one has been together with them in church. Depending on their skills and interest, migrant Others could also help in church meetings, in some cases belonging before believing.

The traditional model of a missionary going abroad to preach the gospel in a foreign country involves full-time ministers who have undergone specialised training in Christian doctrine and the language and culture of the so-called target people. The more centripetal nature of migrant ministry means that host country Christians involved often have full-time secular jobs and lack specialised missionary training and therefore may work with migrants in the same way as with their own countrymen. In addition, differences in income, status, work and living circumstances mean that ministry among migrants is demanding and difficult. Churches need to be serious about appropriate training, networking with other like-minded players, and making use of missionaries with experience in the migrants' home countries.

Ministry to Migrants at the Home End of the Transnational Space

Having looked at practical ministry to migrants in their host countries, it now remains to consider the extension and follow-up to such ministry among those who have returned to their home nations.

The transnational space is the virtual connection between a migrant's home and host countries. It links the two together, and constitutes an extension of the migrant's home culture into the host country. However, the same space can also be thought of as an extension of the Christian community in the host countries back into the migrants' home nations. Just as the transnational space is an invasion of migrants' culture into the host nations, so it can also work as an invasion of the church community from the host nation back into the migrants' home. A variation on missionary sending could see Christians from the host society visit frequently or even take up residence at the other end of the transnational space. That is to say, Christians from Korea could work in Indonesia with the specific aim of reaching migrants in the transnational space, assisting returnees and getting to know those about to migrate, and making connections for them at the Korean end. Indonesian Christians could also be stationed at both ends of the transnational space, working in partnership with Korean colleagues and bringing consistency of personnel as well as practical and spiritual care at both ends of the transnational space. These Christian presences dedicated to the needs of migrants could be constituted by professionals, business people, or students, as well as full-time missionaries. A group of European Christians already serves in one Asian country with the specific task of welcoming returnees back into the country, and this is a partial precedent for a similar intra-regional ministry in East Asia.

The flow of migrants within the transnational space also has implications for short-term missions, already popular in East Asia. Rather than have groups of relatively uninformed Christians going to different destinations every year, churches could direct some of their short-term mission effort into the transnational space. Small groups from host country churches could connect with people in a migrant home country, relating to returnees and building friendships with those about to migrate, and challenging stereotypical attitudes on both sides. Where churches do exist in the migrants' home communities, relationships could be built and cooperation and bilateral visits encouraged.

Furthermore, the church can help improve migrants' skills and increase opportunities for them as they return home. Many in the church are highly qualified and work in business, education, and government. This means that there is potential for skills transfer, micro-credit, and the establishment of small and medium-sized enterprises (SMEs) by migrants when they return to their countries. One example of this is the Aidha micro-business school, a not-for-profit training organisation for domestic helpers in Singapore which is now expanding to the Middle East. It takes advantage of Singapore as a global hub and magnet for talented people to equip promising domestic helpers with weekend training and savings schemes. If these women set up businesses, they can sustain themselves and employ others, ending the poverty trap which forces women from poorer nations to work as domestic helpers and potentially sustaining a gospel community which reaches out to Others.

The emphasis on empowerment and escaping from poverty is consistent with the broader Christian message, yet too many churches ministering to Indonesian helpers just offer worship and Bible study. The idea of churches expanding their help to include business training was seen as very positive by domestic helpers who were asked.

Christian equivalents of Aidha and similar projects could aim to establish self-sustaining kingdom presences in migrants' home countries to provide income and bless others spiritually and materially. The idea of Christian workers specifically dedicated to migrant ministry at both ends of the transnational space dovetails with this kind of entrepreneurship training and implementation. Many of the resources for such programmes already exist in churches in the region; it is simply a matter of harnessing them for the insignificant Other. All of this is dependent upon a generous spirit which is happy to invest in those who will ultimately leave the host nation.

A possible extension or spin-off from this kind of thinking would see returning migrants and host Christians establishing recruitment companies specifically for domestic workers and contract labourers. Christian companies could charge lower fees for recruitment of personnel, provide better training for migrant labour on arrival in the host nations, and offer much improved and ethical care for migrant labourers while they are abroad. This general ethos of care for the Other could also integrate Christian themes or evangelistic efforts as appropriate.

Concluding Remarks

This research constitutes a first attempt to produce a theological and missiological response to migration in East Asia. The form of migration and nature of the host societies in Asia are different from those in North America and Europe, where more research has been done.

The work has also examined biblical teaching about migrants and the obligation of the community of faith to them. This was carried out by using the two concepts of Otherness and liminality and the resulting ideas summarised and applied to popular Confucian ideas which underlie the worldview of many Christians in the region. Theological support was derived for ministry to migrant peoples as true cross-cultural mission, particularly by analogy to the expansion process of the early church. There is much more to be done, and further research could pursue one of any number of areas, but it is to be hoped that this research agenda will develop and deepen and ultimately be of use to the church and of benefit to migrant peoples themselves.